Easy Proven Steps To High Performance

How To Achieve Your Potential And Create The Life You Want

Dr. Katherine Humphrey

Table Of Contents

Introduction

Welcome to a journey of transformation, where the ordinary becomes extraordinary and your potential becomes your power. Finding your path to high performance can feel daunting in a world buzzing with noise and distractions. But don't worry; within the pages of this book are the keys to unlocking your real potential.

Have you ever wondered what distinguishes the top achievers from the rest? The secret isn't buried in some elusive realm—it's right here, within your grasp. This book **"Easy Proven Steps To High Performance"** is more than just words on paper; it's a personalized roadmap tailored to navigate the twists and turns of your unique journey. Through easy, proven steps, you'll find yourself on a trajectory toward high performance, unlocking doors you never thought possible.

Embark on a quest to unveil the potential within you, waiting to be awakened.

But why should you embark on this adventure? Because deep within you lies untapped potential, this book is the catalyst that transforms potential into power. Imagine a life where your goals are not mere aspirations but achievable milestones. Visualize waking up every morning with purpose, armed with the tools to conquer challenges and savor victories.

What sets this book apart is its simplicity, yet profound impact. You won't find complicated theories or unreachable ideals here. Instead, discover easy, proven steps that seamlessly integrate into your daily life, transforming the mundane into the extraordinary. It's a personalized approach to high performance, designed to fit your unique journey.

It's time to build a life that genuinely reflects your potential and to throw off the chains of mediocrity. Your journey to high performance starts now, and this book is your compass. Prepare to redefine your limits, surpass expectations, and create the life you've always wanted. The first step is here—let's take it together.

Chapter 1

Understanding Your Current State

Establishing objectives, both personal and professional, can boost output and give you a sense of accomplishment—especially if the objective holds significance for you. Setting realistic goals requires measuring your progress since it lets you prioritize your chores and determine how long they might take to finish. Monitoring your development can also assist you in determining how to modify your action plan, thereby accelerating your advancement.

This chapter will address the significance of progress measurement, and the need to assess your existing situation to determine how to measure it, as well as offer practical examples of how to do so.

Why Is It Necessary to Track Progress?

Once you've established a goal, tracking your advancement will help you reach it. It can assist you in understanding the kinds of activities that advance you and the most efficient approaches.

After that, you can include these techniques in your overarching plan to achieve a certain objective. Assessing your progress can also show you how near you are to reaching a particular objective. This could serve as a helpful reminder of your goals and inspiration to keep moving forward.

How to Track Your Current State

To successfully gauge your progress, think about taking the following actions:

1. Identify what you hope to accomplish.

Determining the action you want to take and the kind of result you're looking for is crucial to creating both long-term and short-term goals. Consider measuring the existing state of a business aspect you intend to enhance to accomplish this efficiently. After that, decide on a clear objective based on that knowledge.

For instance, a business can say that its objective is to have a million social media followers, but it only has 200,000 at the moment. The marketing department of the business might then create precise short- and long-term objectives linked to acquiring 800,000 followers, such as launching an advertisement campaign that specifically targets potential followers. (The same goes for your goal.)

2. Set up a deadline

Setting deadlines for long-term objectives will help you improve the procedures you use to complete short-term jobs. Consider outlining every stage of your approach in writing, along with the amount of time you anticipate needing to complete it, to help you establish a comprehensive strategy. When making plans, think back over the procedures to foresee any issues and prepare fixes. You may find it easier to meet deadlines if you do this to strengthen your time management abilities.

By keeping note of the time and method by which you finish tasks, you can also create a timeline. This can help you reach your long-term objectives by enabling you to review and enhance the techniques you employ to finish assignments. For instance, if a writer signs a book agreement with a publishing house for 100,000 words, the corporation can ask the writer to complete the work in two years. The writer may set short-term objectives, such as writing a certain number of words per day, to track their progress toward their two-year target.

3. Establish milestones

A milestone is a little accomplishment that serves as a gauge for your overall goal's development. Milestones help you visualize every step of your strategy and might give you a sense of satisfaction when you reach them, so they may help you become more focused. Consider selecting a small objective, such as accomplishing a task by a certain date or completing several chores by a given time, to help you design an effective milestone.

Completing all of the courses in a semester could be a significant accomplishment for a college student who wants to teach marine biology. This can assist them in tracking their progress toward their long-term professional objective and estimating the time required to achieve it.

4. Make your Goals SMART

SMART goals are precise, measurable, attainable, relevant, and time-bound objectives. Creating SMART goals will enable you to track your development by:

* Providing precise tasks to monitor: Defining goals and breaking them down into activities can assist you in comprehending the actions required to achieve long-term goals. This might help you determine how long it might take you to accomplish your goals realistically.

* Determining whether your goals are measurable: You should think about utilizing time as a meter to

make sure your goal is measurable. This can be accomplished by creating a timeline, which will assist you in figuring out how many jobs you need to finish, how long you should spend on each work, and how long it might take to accomplish your main objective.

* Ensuring that your goals are attainable: Establishing long-term objectives and employing milestones can assist you in ensuring that your goals are attainable, as certain jobs are simpler to do over an extended period. Assessing the reachability of your objectives might also assist you in deciding if you need to acquire new abilities. After that, you can evaluate your development by keeping note of the abilities you've acquired and the accomplishments of each goal.

* Determining the relevance of your goals: It's useful to assess your goals once you've developed

them to make sure they're appropriate. This can assist you in revising, updating, or adjusting your objectives to ensure that they still meet your demands. Additionally, this can help you organize your time better, which will make it easier for you to gauge your success.

* Developing a time-based action plan outline: By making it simple to see the progress you've made toward a specific goal, creating a timeline can help you measure your success. This might assist you in updating unrealistic deadlines and setting reasonable ones.

5. Record And Evaluate Development

Progress can be effectively measured by recording it. Try keeping a record of your general objectives, assignments, due dates, and milestones. After that, you may use a planner or calendar to keep track of your progress by marking off tasks as you finish them and achievements as you reach milestones. Your planner's information might be able to tell you whether you need to add a new task or modify your timeline.

For instance, a test-taker may utilize a calendar to specify the test date and set a study deadline if their objective is to pass a certification exam with a high score. Then, to keep focused on their long-term objective, they can list the subjects they must study, calculate how much time they should spend studying each day, and establish milestones.

Chapter 2

Unleashing Your Inner Drive The Key to Passion, and Perseverance

What inspires you? What inspires your enthusiasm and lifts your spirits? For me, it's an innate desire to improve, have a positive influence, never stop learning, and leave a lasting impression on the universe. It's the urge to make a difference in the lives of people around me and to be noticed. This chapter will look at what motivates people, how to discover your mission, and how to persevere in the face of difficulty.

We will also talk about how important it is to recognize setbacks as opportunities for growth and to celebrate little victories.

"Motivation is what fuels your beginning. Habit is what keeps you going."

What Is Motivation?

The internal or external energy that spurs us to act, accomplish our goals, and persevere in the face of difficulties is known as motivation. It is the motivation that propels us to change the world and gives us a sense of purpose and resolve every morning. Our objectives, values, and desires are what drive us to be motivated.

How to Discover Your Motivation and Purpose

1. Self-Reflection: Give your ideals, passions, and hobbies some thought. Which pursuits cause you to become distracted? What makes you happy? These hints can help you find your mission.

2. Establish Meaningful Goals: Establish measurable objectives that are consistent with your principles. Your goals become strong motivators when they have meaning.

3. Create A Positive Environment for Yourself: Try to surround yourself with individuals who are encouraging, growth-oriented, and supportive of your goals.

4. Keep Learning: Motivation can come from curiosity and a quest for information. Never stop looking for new and exciting opportunities to learn and experience.

How To Maintain Resilience

1. Accept Challenges: Rather than seeing impediments, see challenges as chances for personal development. Take them in with a cheerful attitude.

2. Seek Support: When faced with hardship, rely on your network of friends, family, and mentors. They can provide direction, inspiration, and a different viewpoint.

3. Remain Adaptable: Resilience depends on flexibility. Be prepared to modify your plans and approaches in the face of obstacles or unanticipated events.

4. Self-Care: Resilience depends on you taking care of your physical and emotional health. Exercise, engage in mindfulness practices, and make sure you get enough sleep.

How to Reward Your Success and Gain Lessons from Your Setbacks

1. Appreciate Little Wins: Honor and appreciate even the tiniest successes. Every stride forward is a step toward your goal, and celebrating your accomplishments keeps you motivated.

2. Accept Failure as a Teaching Opportunity: See failure as a springboard for development. Examine what went wrong, draw lessons from your errors, and apply what you've learned to future endeavors.

3. Retain Perspective: Recall that obstacles are a natural part of every adventure. Allow them to define you. Remain dedicated to your cause and concentrate on your long-term objectives.

Examples Of Finding Your Purpose and Motivation

***. A Strong Passion for Assisting Others:** Let's say you get immense joy from assisting others who are in need. Your goals may center on working in social work, healthcare, or as a volunteer for nonprofits.

The positive difference you make in other people's lives will be your source of motivation.

*. **Artistic Expression:** If you have a passion for the arts, your goal can be to produce and exhibit your artwork. Whether you're an artist in any other medium, like writing, painting, or music, what drives you is the satisfaction you get from expressing yourself and the hope that others may find inspiration or a connection with your work.

* **Environmental Consciousness:** If you have a strong interest in sustainability and the environment, your goal may be to promote eco-friendly behaviors, work in environmental conservation, or inform people about the value of preserving the environment. Making the earth a better, more sustainable place for coming generations is what motivates you.

* **Educational Advocacy:** Your goal may be to work as a teacher, mentor, or champion for educational reform if you have a strong commitment to education and believe in its transformational power. Your conviction that every kid should have access to a high-quality education is what drives you.

*. **Entrepreneur Spirit:** Let's say you possess a strong sense of entrepreneurial motivation. Your goal can be to develop a company or product that eases people's lives or addresses a particular issue. The excitement of creating something from scratch and the desire to create drive you.

* **Family and Relationships:** Your goal may be to be the best friend, partner, or parent you can be if you derive the greatest happiness and contentment from your relationships with family and loved ones. The affection and bond you have with the

individuals who are most important to you serve as your source of motivation.

* **Scientific Curiosity:** If you have a strong interest in research and discovery, one of your goals may be to further knowledge and advancements in the field. Your quest to comprehend and solve the universe's secrets serves as your driving force.

* **Advocating for Social Justice:** If you have a strong belief in equality and social justice, you may want to pursue activism, advocacy, or employment with human rights-focused groups. Your conviction that every person should have access to the same opportunities and rights drives you.

These illustrations show how varied and unique it may be to discover your inspiration and purpose. Finding something that deeply connects with you and is consistent with your interests and values is crucial. As soon as you've identified your purpose, your dedication to it will automatically inspire you to take initiative and have a significant impact.

In summary

Motivating factors such as enthusiasm, tenacity, and motivation light your way as you travel through life. They provide you with the ability to reach your full potential, have a positive influence, and leave a lasting legacy. You'll discover an inner source of power and resolve as you discover your purpose and fan the flames of your motivation.

Little wins and sporadic failures are all part of life's journey. Honor those victories, regardless of how small they may appear. They serve as the foundation for your achievement. Accept setbacks as important teaching moments since they are the bricks that help you move forward.

When you use resilience as your vehicle, purpose as your destination, and motivation as your compass, you can unleash your inner drive and build a life that is worthy of celebration as well as worth living. Your path, as special and significant as it is, may affect the world in ways you are not yet aware of.

Chapter 3

Cultivating a Growth Mindset

A growth mindset can change how we face difficult business problems and failures, which will increase our success and pleasure.

There might be competition in the world. It takes more than simply tougher work to stay ahead; you also need to work smarter.

The growth mindset can help with that.

In most cases, it is not a reflection on their abilities or efforts when someone in a fast-paced, highly competitive sector isn't accomplishing their objectives or setting the correct priorities. It's usually the result of not having a growth attitude.

You can progressively ascend to greater heights in your career with a growth mindset by only changing the way you think and live.

You're positioning yourself for a deep comprehension of the growth mindset by reading this chapter. I'm going to assist you in defining it, showing you how to develop it, and outlining its advantages for leadership and the company.

What Is A Growth Mindset?

The growth mindset is a way of thinking that supports the notion that intelligence and skill can be acquired with patience, hard work, and devotion. With persistence and time, all of these elements of yourself are capable of development, evolution, and improvement. A growth mindset is an outlook that values resilience, learning from mistakes, and personal development.

Carol Dweck, a psychologist, initially presented this compelling viewpoint through her thorough studies on motivation, success, accomplishment, and mindset.

Dweck's research indicates that the idea of a "growth mindset" is a radical departure from the conventional "fixed mindset." People who have a fixed mindset think that their skills are fixed and unalterable. This may impede personal development and lead to self-imposed barriers.

People who have a growth mentality, on the other hand, welcome challenges, regard failure as a necessary step toward mastery, and think they have limitless potential. Setbacks don't stop them; instead, they view them as stepping stones toward development and mastery. They know that talent and intelligence are malleable. It matters how much work you're willing to put in to develop and progress, not just what you were born with.

The value of a growth mindset is in its ability to enable you to become the best version of yourself, regardless of where you are in your journey.

Why Is It Vital To Nurture A Growth Mindset?

A growth mindset is essential to cultivate since it promotes resilience, eases learning, and ignites success. It promotes the idea that obstacles are opportunities to grow in flexibility and problem-solving skills. Growth-minded people are aware that to succeed, they must push beyond their comfort zone, work hard, and learn from their mistakes.

A growth mentality can change how you handle obstacles and failures, which can increase your success and contentment. It's not only about your thoughts; it's also about your actions and responses to the different circumstances life throws at you. You may perceive the opportunity for progress in every event if you have a mindset that is centered on learning and development.

Can One Develop a Growth Mindset?

Of course! A growth mindset is a perspective that may be developed and fostered over time rather than an innate one.

To cultivate a growth mentality, you must consciously change the way you view obstacles, work, and criticism. Its main idea is that intelligence and aptitude are flexible qualities that can be refined through hard work and dedication. Furthermore, it's about believing in oneself and identifying possibilities for learning and improvement in every circumstance.

Recognizing the existence of a "fixed mindset" and learning how it shows up are the first steps toward developing a growth mindset. It could manifest as an aversion to difficulties, fear of failing, self-limiting beliefs, or a negative response to criticism. You can begin to consciously change your attitude if you can identify these times.

For example, if you are presented with a challenging task, ask yourself:

"What can I learn from this situation?"

"How can I grow from this?"

Step-by-Step Guide For Developing A Growth Mindset

You agree that having a growth mindset is a good concept. You are eager to take advantage of the chances it can present since you see its potential and revolutionary power.

But how can one genuinely develop a growth mindset?

Making the transition from a fixed to a progressive mentality is not as simple as turning on a light switch. It's a journey that calls for thinking, practice, and deliberate effort. The good news, though? It's totally doable, and we have nine tried-and-true methods to guide you.

1. Identify Traps in Fixed Mindsets

Understanding the fixed mindset, which is the opposite of the development mindset, is the first step toward cultivating the latter. These are deep-rooted notions that your skills are fixed and unalterable. Have you ever encountered a weakness or shortcoming in yourself and said to yourself, "Well, that's just the way I am," or have you ever overcome a challenge and said, "That's just the way things are"? You can actively decide to take on a more adaptable mindset by marking these and seeing them as chances for development.

2. Accept Challenges

Accepting challenges in your life is a crucial step in your journey. When faced with obstacles, a person who has a growth mindset sees them as chances to improve and learn rather than as obstacles to be overcome. Modify your viewpoint. Consider every obstacle as a riddle to be solved, a mystery to be solved, or a contest to win. The idea is to change the mindset from "I can't do this" to "I can't do this, yet." To improve, always remember that you must challenge yourself, get out of your comfort zone, and dare to do things you once believed were unachievable.

3. Have No Fear of Failing

What comes next? Rethink what failure means. Failure is not viewed as a dead end by those who have a growth mindset. Rather, they see it as a teaching moment – a stepping stone toward achievement. Failure is a sign of bravery for daring to try, not of inability. Don't let failure demoralize you the next time. Examine what went wrong, draw lessons from it, and apply what you've learned to improve the next time.

4. Value the Effort

Realize that the force behind progress is effort. Your work isn't in vain even when it feels like it's taking a while; it's helping you develop the fortitude and perseverance you'll need to reach your objectives. Establish clear, attainable goals that will take work to accomplish, and monitor your progress to make sure your efforts are going where they will have the biggest impact. It will be reaffirmed that skills may be developed and enhanced with time and effort if hard work and perseverance are valued and celebrated.

5. Keep Learning

A growth mindset's cornerstone is a strong desire to learn new things. It involves having a never-ending curiosity, looking for new information all the time, and working tirelessly to get better. Make an effort to see every day as a chance to learn something new. Accept the thrill of learning, whether it's picking up a new skill for your job, exploring a subject you've always been curious about, or even learning a tasty new recipe.

6. Foster Solidity

Growth mindsets are fueled by persistence. It's the determination to press on through difficult times. When faced with obstacles, people with a growth mentality consistently lean into the discomfort rather of pulling back into the safety of the familiar. It's second nature to them.

The key to perseverance with a development mindset is realizing that significant accomplishments take time and work. It's about valuing the process rather than just the result, and enjoying the trip as much as the destination. It promotes a positive outlook on failure, seeing obstacles as helpful learning opportunities and essential components of personal development rather than as the end of the path.

7. Seek Out Constructive Feedback

Adopting a growth mindset requires the capacity to take constructive criticism and act upon it. It offers an external viewpoint that can draw attention to blind spots and development potential. Feedback is not a personal jab; rather, it's a tool for personal development.

Cultivating a growth mindset requires learning to actively seek out and be open to constructive criticism. Seek for coworkers, coaches, or mentors who can offer you frank criticism. Make use of their feedback to hone your tactics, develop your abilities, and propel yourself forward.

8. Keep A Company Of Growth-Minded Individuals

Your company makes you who you are. Encountering others who share a growth mentality can significantly influence your path. Their upbeat outlooks, strength in the face of adversity, and unwavering dedication to personal development can inspire and motivate you. Additionally, they can offer priceless guidance, support, and inspiration while you forge your own route toward development.

9. Celebrate Your Small Victories As Well As The Successes Of Others

Accepting a development mentality means not seeing other people's success as a threat but as a source of inspiration. Honor the successes of your colleagues and think about the lessons they have to teach you. You can grow with them by seeing how they achieved a goal, the tactics they used, and how they might be applied or modified to your own circumstances. Finding inspiration in your environment is a wonderful and fulfilling experience.

Above all, remember to enjoy every tiny victory and accomplishment you achieve! Don't minimize yourself because you see people with more accomplishments than you. You will have the strength to press on if you are grateful for your steady progress.

Embrace the Power of a Growth Mindset: Your Adventure Begins Now

Adopting a growth mindset can have profound personal and professional transformations. Having a growth mindset gives you the willpower to overcome obstacles, the fortitude to pick yourself up after failing, and the drive to pursue your goals.

You can conquer the world like never before thanks to the power of a development mentality.

Recall that you are on a path toward growth.

Obstacles present chances for development. Accept them.

Failure does not mean loss. It's an educational opportunity.

Mastery is reached via effort.

Encourage a love of lifelong study.

Seek out and value-helpful criticism.

Put yourself in the company of growth-oriented people.

You're laying the groundwork for boundless career and personal development by putting these techniques into practice. Recall that developing and maintaining a growth mindset requires work. Although this path isn't always simple, it's one of the most fulfilling experiences you can have. Now take a deep breath, venture beyond your comfort zone, and immerse yourself in the growth mindset community. Your future self will be appreciative.

Chapter 4

Setting Appropriate Goals For Your Life To Achieve Maximum Well-Being

It can be difficult to strike the correct balance between different facets of life in the fast-paced, high-demanding world of today. It's simple to lose sight of what is important and to disregard our mental and emotional health as our to-do list grows. On the other hand, setting sensible priorities for our lives can result in a happier and more satisfying life.

Ten doable and tested strategies to manage your life priorities and improve your general well-being are covered in this chapter.

1. Reflect Your Goals and Values.

To begin the process of setting priorities in life, consider your long-term objectives and guiding principles. Think about what is important to you, what makes you happy, and what you hope to achieve in the future. You will acquire clarity and be able to better match your activities with your goals and values by going through this introspective process.

2. Establish an Individual Mission Statement

Creating a personal mission statement can be an effective tool for directing your choices and activities in life. It serves as a compass, helping you to maintain focus on the important things in life. Compose a succinct statement that sums up your beliefs, mission, and ultimate aspirations. As you develop and mature, go back to this statement often and make adjustments.

3. Set Explicit Priorities

After you have a firm grasp of your mission and values, it is critical to establish measurable goals for yourself. Decide which aspects of your life need the greatest work, then focus your time and energy there. Recall that it's acceptable to decline engagements or activities that conflict with your priorities.

4. Strengthen Your Capacity To Say No.

Learning to say no is one of the hardest yet most important components of setting priorities in life. Being social creatures, we frequently feel pressure to fulfill obligations to others or accept new duties, even when they conflict with our top goals. Establish boundaries and learn how to graciously turn down offers of assistance that don't align with your greater goals.

5. Make Time Management and Mindfulness Practises

When combined with efficient time management, mindfulness can significantly improve life priorities. Develop an awareness of how you spend your time and live in the present moment. Make progress in all significant aspects of your life by allocating time for your priorities using tools like calendars, to-do lists, and time-blocking tactics.

6. Adopt A Balanced Work-Life

Keeping a good work-life balance is essential to general well-being. As you work towards your goals and profession, don't forget to schedule time for friends, family, hobbies, and self-care. Reaching this equilibrium will improve your happiness and productivity while lowering stress.

7. Develop Truly Meaningful Connections

Having good connections is essential to living a happy life. Make the time and effort to establish and maintain relationships with loved ones, family, and friends. Your mental and emotional health is positively impacted by the love, support, and sense of belonging that these relationships offer.

8. Make Self-Care a Priority

Taking care of yourself is vital, not just a luxury. It's critical to put your mental, emotional, and physical health first by doing things that make you feel refreshed. A healthy diet, regular exercise, getting enough sleep, and participating in hobbies are all crucial aspects of self-care.

9. Limit Distractions

Distractions abound in the digital environment we live in, which makes it difficult to maintain our priorities in mind. Cut back on the amount of time you spend on social media, excessive screen time, and other distractions that impede your ability to be productive and interact with people.

10. Be Adaptable and Welcome Change

Because life is unpredictable, things might change. Accept adaptability and be willing to rearrange your priorities as necessary. Acquire the ability to adjust to novel situations and chances while adhering to your main principles and objectives.

**

Setting priorities in life is a continuous process that calls for flexibility, self-control, and self-awareness. You can live a more balanced and meaningful life by considering your values, prioritizing your tasks, engaging in mindfulness exercises, and valuing self-care. Never forget that it's acceptable to ask friends, family, or professional resources for assistance when you need it. Hold fast to your goals and don't be scared to adjust as you go. A life that supports your priorities gives you a sense of fulfilment, and promotes your general well-being may be achieved with dedication and attention.

Setting priorities in life is about making deliberate decisions that support your values and long-term objectives, rather than trying to be flawless. You can live a more fulfilling and meaningful life and more easily overcome the challenges of modern living by implementing these ten strategies into your daily routine.

Never forget that you are in charge of molding your life and building a future that truly represents your goals and values.

Chapter 5

Hacks For Maximum Productivity

What Does Productivity Mean?

Being productive goes beyond just accomplishing your goals and crossing items off your to-do list. Being productive entails concentrating solely on completing crucial tasks. Do not give up; instead, take one constructive step at a time. The path to increased productivity can be lengthy.

The Significance of Productivity

One of the key factors that will determine both your career success and personal satisfaction may be your productivity. People can progress in their careers and personal lives if they can continuously generate high-quality work at a sustainable rate.

Productivity growth offers the chance to raise production without adding more inputs or corresponding expenses. Since 1947, the US corporate sector has been able to generate nine times more goods and services with a relatively smaller increase in hours worked, according to US Bureau of Labor Statistics data on productivity growth.

Being productive allows you to live the life of your dreams by helping you prioritize work, effectively manage time and resources, and free up time for more fulfilling pursuits.

Top Productivity Hacks to Boost Productivity

1. Plan Your Day Ahead Of Time

Creating a schedule for the day in preparation is the first step toward being productive. On any given day, you ought to be aware of what you're doing, when you're doing it, and for how long. If you don't have a schedule, you'll probably forget to do crucial things.

Either the night before or early in the morning, make a detailed plan for the day. To help you stay on track and know what to work on next, write down everything that has to be done. Because there is no longer any room for speculation, there is less possibility that you will stray from the task at hand and waste time wondering what to do next.

2. List The Top Three Daily Tasks That Are Most Important.

List the top three things you need to get done today. Provide a thorough description of the tasks to remove any doubt. Give priority to significant tasks over urgent ones.

3. Implement Any Productivity Technique

Use a productivity approach to increase your output. Using a very effective productivity tool might help you maintain concentration while working. Using a productivity strategy, you can organize your day by creating attainable objectives. Choose a productivity strategy that works for you and will help you produce more each day.

4. Pick One Goal For Each Day

For each workday, set a single objective to help you concentrate on certain tasks. Dividing daily objectives into smaller, more manageable tasks that you will focus on within the designated time is a smart approach.

5. Designate Specific Times for Email Checks

One of the biggest distractions throughout the workday that wastes time is reading emails. Decide to check your email twice a day, ideally before lunch and before you end the workday.

6. Use More Red and Blue Colors

Clear your desk of any clutter. Red is thought to enhance attention to detail, while blue is known to stimulate creativity, according to studies on the benefits of red and blue hues on brain function. Use these hues all around your workspace to increase output.

7. The Rule Of Two Minutes For Little Tasks

Spend less time debating whether to complete the little chores that keep coming up during the day. Alternatively, ask yourself if you can finish the activity in two minutes or less. If the answer is yes, then proceed with the task. If not, put the task on your list of things to accomplish.

8. Listen To Productive Music

Music therapy is a great way to keep focused and productive. Select music that helps you concentrate on the current task.

9. Make Regular Tasks Using Templates

Make templates for repetitive jobs that must be completed in the same manner each time. You will become more productive overall and save a ton of time by doing this.

10. Refrain From Multitasking

Although it may be tempting to multitask, doing two activities at once is not as beneficial as it seems. 98% of people, according to research, are less effective when they multitask since they are not concentrating on a single task.

11. Choose An Easy or Tough Task To Begin Your Day

The way you begin your day determines how the rest of it goes. Either begin with the most difficult activity so that everything else seems easier, or begin with the simplest task to obtain important momentum.

12. Apply The "One and Done" Rule

The majority of us tend to put off some tasks, believing that we will take care of them later. But because we won't put things on our to-do lists, we hardly ever complete them later. Make a to-do list for every new assignment to ensure you don't forget it later.

13. Take Regular Breaks

You must make the most of breaks to offer your mind the much-needed opportunity to recuperate from prolonged periods of attention. During breaks, fully relax or practice meditation to help your body and mind unwind.

14. Endeavour To Wake Up Early

You feel completely re-energized at the start of a day, which can offer you a wonderful head start on any workday. Early in the morning, when there are fewer distractions than at lunchtime, you can accomplish a lot of work.

15. Ensure That Each Task Is Associated With A Goal.

Make sure a task is connected to a long-term objective, such as one of your SMART goals, before beginning it. If the task has no bearing on your career progression, get rid of it or give it to someone else.

16. Adhere To Deadlines

No matter how much time you have to finish a task, make sure you finish it within the allotted time. Knowing that a deadline is coming up will increase your productivity.

17. Quit Trying To Be Perfect

Don't waste time attempting to make every task perfect because there is nothing perfect. Proceed to the next task if the work meets the necessary standards.

18. Determine The "Why" of Your Work

Consider the reasons behind your decision to pursue the particular field. When working, remember those factors to help you stay motivated to be successful and productive at work.

Chapter 6

Turning Setbacks Into Comebacks

A Fantastic Comeback Story

One of the most amazing comeback tales in history was presented during the 2018 Olympics! On the opening lap of the Men's 30 30-kilometer cross-country Skiathlon, Norwegian Simen Hegstad Krueger went down. Just a few moments into the competition, Krueger's right ski seemed to give way under him, causing him to fall to the ground. There was no time to change direction with two skiers directly behind.

It seemed to everyone watching that his chances of winning an Olympic medal were gone.

When Krueger found himself face down in the snow with two opponents on top of him, he had to decide quickly how to respond. It would have been easy for him to give up and raise his arms. If he had said it wasn't his fault, conceded that a broken pole had caused his defeat, or said he was hurt after being struck in the head, nobody would have held him responsible. He decided to keep trying rather than give up!

He stated in an interview that he had to make an effort to push those unfavorable ideas away. "I was aware that it would be challenging."

He was aware that gaining back the lost fifteen seconds and maintaining sufficient energy for the finish line would require perseverance. Taking a new pole from one of the Norwegian coaches, he made his way through the course slowly, and with five kilometers left, he took the lead.

His realization that his worst adversary could be his negative thoughts was the most impressive aspect of his recovery. He was able to make up for lost time and seize the money by forcing them from his thoughts as soon as possible.

Setbacks

Everyone has been there. Even though it wasn't in front of millions of spectators during the Olympics, we have all tripped, fallen, and suffered a setback. Everybody has different stresses and difficulties to deal with, some of which seem overwhelming at times. It can be challenging to remember to ignore the bad and concentrate on what is achievable.

When anything seems to be impeding your development, it's called a setback. Though it could appear challenging or less probable, it is not a failure.

It just implies that to recover and grow from our experience, we must be resourceful.

It's possible that something doesn't go as expected or that you had hoped for. Sometimes finding a fresh solution requires starting over from scratch. a distinct perspective to develop a new strategy.

A minor setback, like suffering a migraine on a hectic day, might have a significant impact, like tripping and falling during a gold medal attempt. In any case, it's critical to keep in mind that obstacles are just temporary.

Comebacks

Watching friends or relatives overcome obstacles can be tough, especially if it has nothing to do with you. Gaining the ability to manage these kinds of circumstances and recover is an important life skill.

1. Keep Track of Your Response

Anger, fear, and frustration are all typical emotions linked to the difficulty of a setback. None of these unfavorable responses, though, will assist you in making your next move. I've discovered that although I can't ignore these emotions, I can swiftly put them in the back of my thoughts after I've acknowledged them. Positive ones can now replace negative ones as a result. Recall the tiny engine with great potential.

2. Defeat is just Temporary

You make the decisions about what is temporary and what is permanent since you are the ship's master. It is totally up to you to make any adjustments to your motivation, attitude, or conduct. Only when we give up do we acknowledge the loss.

Being defeated is frequently an ephemeral state. What makes it permanent is giving up.-Marilyn Vos Savant

3. Don't Waste Time Blaming

When I think about who is to blame, I usually think back to when I was younger and got caught doing something wrong. When my mother would question me about why I did something, I would always say, "She made me do it," gesturing to the nearest person.

Blaming someone else instead of oneself is a normal reaction to feelings of guilt and humiliation. It eases the immediate pain of making a mistake and offers some consolation to our conscience. It is a waste of time to point fingers, offer reasons, or ask, "WHY ME?" It turns away from what counts, which is how to keep moving forward. Blame can become a bigger roadblock than the real one.

4. Always remember to ask for Help.

The Savior is constantly thinking of you, no matter what. He recognizes your efforts, knows what you need, and is waiting for you on the sidelines to give you a new, undamaged pole. You will gain assurance that tomorrow will be better as you work to remember and obey Him today.

Conclusions

Remaining persistent and processing your emotions is crucial to any recovery, regardless of the severity of the setback. After a taste of defeat or failure, redoubling your efforts to succeed will get you across the finish line. Above all, we never get lost. No matter how dismal things seem in our lives, there is always someone waiting to support and encourage us.

Chapter 7

Sustaining Success Over The Long Term

"Vision without execution is just hallucination." — *Henry Ford*

Since success is based on compound interest, there are no shortcuts to getting there. It is the result of numerous tiny efforts put out over time. Like most individuals, you have dreams that you hope will come true in the future. But in the absence of dedication, organization, and clarity, they probably will stay that way.

It's a difficult path from dream to reality. Not everyone is suited for it.

However, one can get an advantage by studying some of the methods and approaches employed by those who have already done so.

The four strategies listed below can assist you in achieving long-term, steady success. They accomplish this by assisting you in setting high standards, demanding deadlines, and the concentration needed to work consistently.

1. Establish Specific Goals With This 3-Step Process

It's easier than ever for us to lose sight of our objectives right now. Because distractions are the largest issue that most people have when attempting to succeed.

Our culture is designed to divert our attention. We receive notifications asking us to check our phones more than 200 times a day, in addition to the never-ending 24-hour news cycle.

You will likely have a wide range of interests if you consider yourself to be creative. It's common to lose several hours a day reading the newest blog post, watching that new TV show, or searching the internet for inspiration.

We need to be crystal clear about our objectives to keep ourselves from straying. Possibly even more crucially, we must understand what our objectives are not.

This provides us with a simple method to gauge any activity:

Does it help me achieve goal X or does it get in the way of it?

I follow a three-step procedure to make sure my goals are clear. Warren Buffet, a millionaire investor, employs this strategy. You could do it today since it's so easy. This is how it operates.

Step 1: List your top 25 objectives. These could be your weekly objectives, professional aspirations, or even personal aspirations. Depending on your goals, yes.

Step 2: Go over the list and mark the top five objectives.

Note: Before proceeding to step 3 below, pause and finish steps 1 and 2 if you are truly doing this.

STEP 3: There are now two lists. List A is the five-item list. List B is the 20-item list.

What distinguishes the two lists, then?

These are your top five priorities in List A. As much time as you can go into accomplishing these five objectives.

Your "avoid-at-all-costs" items are in List B. It is best to consciously refrain from devoting any time or effort to achieving these goals.

Now that you have a blueprint for success, it is critical to ascertain the exact moment at which you wish it to occur.

2. Establish a Set Deadline for Each Goal

Not having an endpoint for a goal is one of the biggest mistakes most people make when they set one. If you don't have a specific deadline to strive for, all you're doing is daydreaming.

Give a deadline for each of your top five objectives to be accomplished. You'll see that this makes you more explicit about the goals you have in mind.

This year, I wanted to "lose weight." However, that was overly ambiguous.

I have to set a precise aim for myself in addition to an endpoint.

Thus, "get fit" became "lose 9.5 kg by August 30." I was able to transform a general aim into a specific one by setting a deadline for myself.

You feel more pressure when there is a set date. Additionally, it gives you a timeline structure so you can schedule the actions you need to execute at the appropriate times. It's acceptable for your endpoint to change if something unforeseen occurs because reality can be messy. But before you can begin, you must drive a stake into the ground.

As commitment is what drives behavior, the objective is to instill a sense of commitment.

3. Set Ambitious and Outstanding Goals

Although it might seem contradictory, a 100% success rate is not a good thing. A good aim is sufficiently ambitious to suggest an achievement barrier of 60–70%.

Some of the most successful people on the planet employ a strategy known as "stretch goals." Every quarter, Google, the second most valuable business in the world, asks its staff to set stretch objectives. This is their explanation of the concept:

Stretch objectives are difficult to create since they run the risk of making a team look bad. But more often than not, these kinds of objectives draw the greatest talent and produce the most stimulating work environments. Furthermore, when one aims high, even unfulfilled ambitions often lead to significant progress.

You're not being ambitious enough if you routinely accomplish 100% of your goals. You're being cautious and leaving wins on the table. This is not an exam from school where you receive points for answering each question correctly. The secret to producing "moonshots" is to dream bigger than you are comfortable with.

Setting somewhat ambitious goals forces you to push yourself to reach new heights in performance. That occasionally implies that you have to make do with only reaching 70%. Sometimes, though, you'll surprise yourself by hitting a huge home run.

Big wins are difficult to achieve if you don't have high goals.

4. Limit Yourself to Six Tasks Each Day (and You'll Get More Done)

Things can get chaotic when you're attempting to create a side business, raise a family, and hold down a career. There are so many things to do every day, even if it's just your day job. However, "being busy" is a certain way to never finish any task.

You are well aware that being busy is a fiction and a trap. Do not play the busy card, please. — Godin, Seth

Yes, there are times when we all feel overextended. However, lacking a precise framework to approach your workload results in being busy. You can only accomplish so much each day, so it's critical to focus on the truly necessary things.

You should now have a distinct set of lofty objectives with a determined completion date. The next stage is to start putting ideas into practice by doing at least one thing every day. Using the Ivy Lee approach is one of the easiest and most efficient ways to accomplish this.

The Ivy Lee story is well-known (if you're not familiar with it already, read up on it), but the basic idea behind the strategy is this:

* Prioritize your list of the six most important tasks you have to complete today.

* Begin working on the first, and don't start on the second until the first is finished.

* Proceed through the entire list in this manner, completing as many items as you can.

* Write your list for the following day when the day is over. To get back to six, carry over any unfinished work and add new ones.

It's among the simplest methods of increasing productivity that I've found. I've been able to double my production, though. Avoid multitasking. Avoid sending emails during the day. Absence of outside interference. Just one thing at a time.

This method is excellent since it makes you carefully consider which chores to include on your list and in what order. Always ask yourself if a task advances your five goals or takes your attention away from them. Steer clear of the latter. Give the former priority.

If you don't know where the goalposts are, you can't score. I've been a writer for more than a year. During that period, I worked nearly every day. But because I didn't know why I was doing it, a lot of it was time squandered. It has taken me nearly a full year to identify my goals, the reason I write, and the deadline by which I hope to accomplish them.

Now that I have a structure to work within, my everyday existence is so much simpler. Additionally, I'm seeing considerably higher returns on my energy investments. since I now know exactly which way to go.

It is considerably simpler to strike your objective when you know what you're going for.

Whatever your concept of success may be, you'll need a strong base to work from. You can accomplish that with the aid of these methods. The remaining aspects require discernment to avoid rushing, self-control to maintain consistency, and persistence to persevere.

Other Books Written By This Author

*Who Says You Can't Flirt As A Woman?: Master The Art of Connection In The Digital Age And Rediscover Your True Self

*How to Transform Insecure Attachment Patterns and Unlock the Key to Deeply Satisfying Relationships (A Comprehensive Guide)